Nation of Islam Decoded
Sciences of Mankind

by

Rasheed L. Muhammad

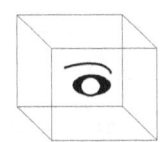

R.L.M. Publishing

Dedicated to the early Pioneers

and

Future Generations

First Edition 2007

(Under the title "Message To The Nation of Islam in North America")

Second Edition 2008

Third Edition 2009

Table of Content

Forward

Nation of Islam Decoded: Sciences of Mankind unlock the fields of study contained in the Secret Lessons given to members of the Nation of Islam in 1930 by its founder, Wallace Fard Muhammad. The people to whom he first divulged these *Secret Lessons* resided in Detroit, Michigan in an area once known as "Black Bottom". Some say "Paradise Valley." Nevertheless, Detroit, Michigan is where the Nation of Islam had its beginning in North America.

Wallace Fard Muhammad first entered North America in 1910 as a foreign exchange student. He was born in Mecca, Arabia on February 26, 1877. His father was a jet black Afro-Asiatic and his mother was a Caucasian woman of the caucus regions of Europe. One of the main aspects of Fard's message identified Black people of America as "lost and found Asiatic" inhabitants of the earth.

According to the Nation of Islam's (N.O.I.) history, he taught thousands of people many sciences of civilization and also renamed 25,000 people giving them Muslim names to replace their European/Christian slave names. This took place over a period of four years from 1930 to 1934. Then suddenly he vanished as rumor had it during that time. In 1934, before making his departure, however, he chose one of his most trustworthy converts or registered Muslim students to lead and maintain the foundation of the Nation he had initiated. That student was named Elijah Poole who later was given the last name Muhammad, thus Elijah Muhammad was commissioned by Fard to inculcate the *"lost and found Asiatics"* of America with the sciences of how to govern themselves, as a nation, within the hostile political environment of Anglo-American Financial oligarchs.

There is nothing illegal about establishing a nation within a nation. According to Wikipedia, the free encyclopedia: A nation is a human cultural and social community. In as much as most members never meet each other, yet feel a common bond, it may be considered an imagined community. One of the most influential doctrines in Western Europe and the Western hemisphere since the late eighteenth century is that all humans are divided into groups called nations. And so, Elijah Muhammad along with being commissioned by Fard to establish a nation, was given the entire production of the *Secret Lessons* typically described as The Supreme Wisdom Book—a book containing six sets of lessons. Its contents entire text has been posted on the Internet, yet without liberating its marvelous message. Astonishingly, the esoteric meanings of these lessons reveal the ologies or fields of scientific study and action needed by all nations of people to build real wealth, security, public health and safety. You may ask what is ology.

Simply put: ology or logy denotes a field of study or academic discipline and ologist describes a person who studies that field. Also, -ology is sometimes used to describe a subject rather than the study of it. If Black people of America, descendants of the Atlantic slave trade are to gain bona fide respect, they must apply the science of ologies to build real wealth to propel themselves into the 21st century with surefire offspring. The success of such national and international endeavor begins with love, family, hard work and the implementation of academic discipline.

This book demonstrates how The Supreme Wisdom Books esoteric message relates to every applied science used in the modern world today.

Although the esoteric nature of its language was light years ahead of where the typical "Black" Muslim follower comprehended in 1930, nevertheless its contents affected their actions in the world around them toward improvement. It moved them near economic, social and political self-determination beyond Anglo-American psy-ops control. In particularly, from 1960 to 1975 when black conscious movements went beyond where America's post slavery/Jim Crow era had discouraged black consciousness. Fact is mainstream America first became aware of the N.O.I. when it gained media prominence after a 1959 documentary by Mike Wallace and Louis Lomax. This documentary presented their interpretation of the rise of Black Nationalist which featured the rise of the "Lost and Found members of the The Nation of Islam".

Who are the Lost and Founds? They are the descendants of West Africans brought to South America, North America and the Caribbean Islands, including Haiti as slaves. These Asiatic originals of West Africa were brought into the Western hemisphere, as slaves, beginning in 1501 and became lost after enduring centuries of brutal slave labor. In terms of their tribal identities, the slaves originated from Senegal, Chad, Ghana, Mali, Jenne, Morocco, Yoruba, Bariba, Sierra Leona, Benin, Gambia, Angola, Nigeria and Guinea. They once knew themselves as the Hausa, Oyo or Nago, Ewe, Moors, Wolof, Tukulor, Mandingo, Fulani, Susu, Mina, Nupe, Futa, Bundu, Jallon and Toro.[1]   However, today in particularly, Blacks of North America have been known to refer to themselves as Colored, Negro, and know not what.

---

[1] Read "Servants of Allah: African Muslims Enslaved in the Americas," by Sylviane A. Diouf.

The question becomes: Is it possible for Black America to produce, rear and guide their offspring to nationhood i.e., doctors, surgeons, lawyers, engineers, land developers, geologist, anthropologist, mathematicians, theologians, Linguist, stock market bankers, investment bankers, gastronomist, geneticist, historians, scientist, meteorologist, oceanography, sociologist, agriculturist, horticulturist, industrious, manufacturers, physiologist and the like. Or are Black children and their parents too distracted under the influence of gadgetry, fashion, entertainment, sport and play and a voracious consumption chasing the "bitch god."[2] Whatever the case might be, this book *"Nation of Islam Decoded: Sciences of Mankind"* is a blueprint for generations to come.

Anthony L. Muhammad
February 17, 2006
[Edited February 25, 2009]

---

[2] Materialism

Chapter 1

Actual Facts

Accounting to the instructions given to those who want to labor for Islam, Wallace Fard Muhammad wrote: *"Assignment of Office will be made immediately after Examination, and on Completion of his or her Labor Course. Consideration for the Laborers of Islam will be taken, and Analysis, in the near future by ALLAH! NOTE: THIS PARAGRAPH puts a stop to all Quarreling and Arguments among the Laborers over their Offices in ISLAM until he or she have been qualified and their qualification Examined to see if they are Fit to be used in the Respective Position."*

The first set of lessons of the Supreme Wisdom Book is described as Actual Facts. A total of 20 are enumerated in this lesson. All of them were to be memorized and ultimately acted upon by registered Muslims of the N.O.I. Samples of a few Actual Facts are offered below to demonstrate only the ologies or fields of study contained in what Wallace Fard Muhammad gave to Elijah Muhammad and the early Muslims during the 1930's.

Actual Facts

The area of the Land is 57,255,000 miles

The producing land is 29,000,000 square miles.

The deserts are 4,861,000 square miles.

The hills and mountains cover 14,000,000 square mile.

Fields of Study (ologies) derived from Actual Facts

Geomorphogeny: Study of the origins of land forms
Agronomics: Study of productivity of land
Agrology: Study of agricultural soils
Agrostology: Science or study of grasses
Geoponics: Study of agriculture
Edaphology: Study of soils
Eremology: Study of deserts
Phytology: Study of plants; botany
Orology: Study of mountains
Mineralogy: Study of minerals

The wealth of industries and services derived from the above fields of study of the Actual Facts are breathtaking. For instance, if one were to put into operation agrology (study of agricultural soils) or geoponics (study of agriculture) commerce, trade, economics and jobs will naturally evolve. Such fundamental developments represent the basis to sustain life and governments. For all practical intent and purpose, the sciences derived from the Actual Facts require academic obedience that lends to wealth building opportunities as seen below for a people who will to produce offspring of fulfillment.

Animal Aquaculture
Animal Specialities
Animal Specialty Services, Except Veterinary
Beef Cattle Feedlots
Beef Cattle, Except Feedlots
Berry Crops
Broiler, Fryers, and Roaster Chickens

Cash Grains, NEC
Chicken Eggs
Citrus Fruits
Corn
Cotton
Cotton Ginning
Crop Harvesting Primarily by Machine
Crop Planting, Cultivating and Protecting
Crop Preparation

Services For Market, except Cotton Ginning
Dairy Farms
Deciduous Tree Fruits
Farm Labor Contractors and Crew Leaders
Farm Management Services
Farm Supplies
Farm-Product Raw Materials
Field Crops, Except Cash Grains
Food Crops Uncover
Fruits and Tree Nuts
Fur-Bearing Animals and Rabbits
General Farms, Primarily Crop
General Farms, Primarily Livestock and Animal Specialties
General Livestock, Except Dairy and Poultry
Grain and Field Beans
Grapes
Horses and Other Equines
Irish Potatoes

Landscape Counseling and Planning
Lawn and Garden Services
Livestock
Livestock Services, Except Veterinary
Ornamental Floriculture and Nursery Products
Ornamental Shrub and Tree Services
Poultry Hatcheries
Poultry and Eggs
Rice
Sheep and Goats
Soil Preparation Services
Soybeans
Sugarcane and Sugar Beets
Tobacco
Tree Nuts
Turkey and Turkey Eggs
Vegetables and Melons
Veterinary Services For Livestock
Veterinary Services for Animal Specialties
Wheat

G8 nations[3] employed these fields of study centuries ago. Imagine the type of parents, education, research, study; community and dedication, a people need to get benefits for themselves by knowing the

---

[3] The Group of Eight (G8) also known as Group of Seven and Russia, is an international forum for the governments of Canada, France, Germany, Italy, Japan, Russia, the United Kingdom and the United States. Together, these countries represent about 65% of the world economy.

potential of the Actual Facts pertaining to what earth yields! We are not presenting paradoxical mumbo jumbo. The language of the Supreme Wisdom Book is written in many degrees of depth that is being translated into ordinary, understandable language. *(Quran 28:51-53)*

Below are a few more examples of "ologies" contained in the Actual Facts of the N.O.I.'s Supreme Wisdom Book.

Actual Facts

The Atlantic Ocean covers 41,321,000 square miles

The Pacific Ocean cover 68,634, 000 square miles

Lakes and rivers cover 1,000,000 square miles

The area of the water is 139,685,000square miles

Fields of Study (ologies) derived from Actual Facts

Oceanology: Study of oceans
Selenology: Study of the moon
Phycology: Study of algae and seaweeds
Fluviology: Study of watercourses
Picatology: Study of fishes
Potamology: Study of rivers
Hydrography: Study of investigating bodies of water
Ichthytology: Study of fish
Limnobiology: Study of fresh water ecosystems
Limnology: Study of bodies of fresh water
Microanatomy: Study of microscopic tissue
Microbiology: Study of microscopic organisms
Hydrobiology: Study of aquatic organisms

Look at the wealth our waters furnish! According to the Food and Agriculture Organization

(FAO), the world harvest in 2005 consisted of 93.2 million tonnes captured by commercial fishing in wild fisheries, plus 48.1 million tonnes produced by fish farms. In addition, 1.3 million tons of aquatic plants (seaweed etc) were captured in wild fisheries and 14.8 million tons were produced by aquaculture. The fishing industry is the commercial activity aimed at the delivery of fish and other seafood products for human consumption or as input factors in other industrial processes. The fishing industry includes any industry or activity concerned with taking, culturing, processing, preserving, storing, transporting, marketing or selling fish or fish products.[4]

As one continues reading the Actual Facts of the N.O.I., you begin to realize there is no "ology" or science operated by a mystery God. Qualified men and women who have mastered, to some degree fields of study must apply, operate and manage all modernity of human life. Let us hope the days of horse and buggy remain in the past. Man and woman have access from the universe and nature to re-create our convenient needs and wants by imagination, innovation and scientific endeavors.

Actual Facts

Light travels at the rate of 186,000 miles per second.

Sound travels at the rate of 1,120 feet per second.

The Earth is 93,000,000 from the Sun.

The Diameter of the Sun is 853,000 Miles.

---

[4] Fish Farming from Wikipedia

Fields of Study (ologies) derived from Actual Facts

Optics: Study of light
Dioptrics: Study of light refraction
Acoustics: Science of sound
Catacoustics: Science of echoes or reflected sounds
Heliology: Science of the sun
Horology: Science of time measurement
Horography: Art of constructing sundials or clocks
Calorifics: Study of heat

What business service does the sun offer man in terms of efficiency, savings, profit and renewable energy? USDA has funded more than 400 loans and grants since the renewable energy program began in FY 2003. To date, the Bush Administration has invested through this program nearly $66.7 million in 36 states. This program can assist farmers, ranchers, and small rural businesses develop renewable energy systems and make energy efficiency improvements to their operations. During fiscal year 2006, Texas provided nearly 1.7 million for this program. For further information regarding this program contact the USDA Rural Development... Also research USDA Energy Initiatives.

Solar energy is energy directly from the Sun. This energy drives the climate and weather and supports virtually all life on Earth. Heat and light from the sun, along with solar-based resources such as wind and wave power, hydroelectricity and biomass, account for most of the available flow of renewable energy. The study of the sun and its usage for civilization is ongoing and ever developing.

For instance, in the Arabian city of Masdar, 22 billion dollars is being invested to build a city using the Sun. Masdar City, the world's first zero-carbon city, will look strikingly different from today's urban hubs.

There will be no skyscrapers or cars. Instead, the city will consist of low-rises lined with *solar panels to take advantage of the near-constant sunshine.* It's 50,000 residents will move around the 2.4 square miles of the city a series of transport pods which function much like horizontal elevators. Pedestrians will never be more than 600 feet from transportation and a light railway will transport people to and from Masdar and Abu Dhabi.[5]

United States of Africa

One-day Africa will function as a Union and she too may best use solar energy and renewable energy resources foremost among any continent on earth because of her near-constant access to sunshine. Hopefully this ancient Original Asiatic people will (re) mature to become a G9 or G10 nation and shed itself from dysfunctionality.

In 2006, I personally had the pleasure to spend nineteen days in Senegal, West Africa and some small towns around her. From what I observed, Africa is slowly producing the type of generation[s] who will meet the challenges of the 21st century and beyond. One day, when education is "free" for students on the mother continent, there will be millions qualified with the sciences of nationhood building and intranationalism from a Divine point of view.

The United States of Latin Africa (*Les Etats-Unis de l'Afrique Latine*) was the proposed union of Romance-language-speaking African countries envisioned by Barthélémy Boganda. The idea's implementation was cut short with Boganda's death in a plane crash on March 29, 1959.

---

[5] Source www.hugg.com/taxonomy/term/4854

15

Richard Wright criticised the idea of United States of Latin Africa in a special introduction to French readers of a translation of his book *White Man, Listen!*, on the bases that Latin Africa meant Catholic Africa and that it would create a religious division against secular English speaking Africa which he called Protestant Africa.

It was nearly 50 years later when this concept was advanced again by Libyan leader Muammar al-Gaddafi at a 2000 summit in Lomé, Togo (and again in June 2007), and by Alpha Oumar Konare, chairperson of the African Commission, on the occasion of the commemoration of the Africa Day, on May 25, 2006.

The phrase *"United States of Africa"*, was mentioned first by Marcus Garvey in his poem 'Hail, United States of Africa' in 1924. Garvey's ideas deeply influenced the birth of the Pan-Africanist movement which culminated in 1945 with the Fifth Pan African Congress in Manchester, United Kingdom, attended by W.E.B. Du Bois, Patrice Lumumba, George Padmore, Jomo Kenyatta and Kwame Nkrumah.

The latest meeting of the African Union, which began on July 1, 2007, was called with a purpose of discussing Gaddafi's idea of a federation of African states.[6]

Just think if Africans understood how to govern the related economics—production, distribution and consumption of goods and services—of their cooper, diamonds, gold, natural gas, petroleum, phosphate and timber. This is not just something to think about, it is something that must be done. The rich natural resources of Africa rival those of both Asia and South America in the developing world. Although much lower in freshwater resources, Sub-Saharan Africa's

---

[6] http://en.wikipedia.org/wiki/United_States_of_Africa

quantities of permanent pasture, forest and woodland, and total land mass are substantial. Furthermore, across the spectrum of natural resources, the vast majority remains underutilized. There can be little doubt that future development in African countries is dependent upon or closely linked to sustainable use of natural resources.[7]

What will the elders of Africa do? Time will only tell. What ever they decide, the ologies heretofore must be made available to all her citizenry with as much zeal as a soccer fan has for their favorite team.

---

[7] http://www.naufrp.org/africa/Report.htm

Chapter 2

Student Enrollment Rules of Islam

In the lesson called "Student Enrollment, Rules of Islam", all Nation of Islam members were given knowledge about the first people on earth, and the people who were classified as "Colored". This particular lesson contains 10 questions and 10 answers written by Wallace Fard Muhammad.

Know Thy Self is what one ancient Egyptian scientist proclaimed 4,600 year ago! Success of a person and/or a people seems to come easily to those with pleasing personalities. However, this does not necessarily mean that you need to do what everyone else wishes if you know thy self.

A positive self-attitude begins by knowing the history of man and woman. Such knowledge helps to develop a respectful opinion of others at the same time remaining true to your own beliefs and cultural history. On the other hand, sometimes an explanation may come from historical evidence from whom it is obligatory to reject, or from whom it is necessary to withhold from until further clarification.

Therefore, a few examples of questions and answers of this secret lesson, Student Enrollment, along with its "ologies" (field of study) are presented below. They speak volumes about the discipline, study, research and institutions needed by a people desirous of knowing themselves and gain an understanding of the entire human family of both man and mankind.

Student Enrollment

1. Who is the Original Man?
Answer: The Original Man is the Asiatic Black Man, the Maker, the Owner, the Cream of the Planet Earth, God of the Universe.

2. Who is the Colored Man?
Answer: The Colored Man is the Caucasian (White man) or Yacob's grafted devil, the Skunk of the Planet Earth.

Fields of Study (ologies) derived from Student Enrollment

Ethnogeny: Study of orgins of races or ethnic groups
Anthropology: Study of human cultures
Ekistics: Study of human settlement
Palaeoathropology: Study of early humans
Archology: Science of the origins government

Student Enrollment

3. What is the population of the Original Nation in the Wilderness of North America and all over the Planet Earth?
Answer: The Population of the Original Nation in the wilderness of North America is 17,000,000 with the 2,000,000 Indians make it, 19,000,000. All over the Planet Earth is 4,400,000,000.

4. What is the population of the Colored People in the wilderness of North America and all over the Planet Earth?
Answer: The Population of the Colored People in the wilderness of North America is 103,000,000 million. All over the Planet Earth is 400,000,000.

Fields of Study (ologies) derived from Student Enrollment

Larithmics: Study of population statistics

20

Sociology: Study of society
Geotechnics: Study of increasing habitability of the earth

Student Enrollment

6. How much of the useful land is used by the Original Man?
Answer: The Original Man uses 23,000,000 square miles.
7. How much of the useful land is used by the Colored Man?
Answer: The Colored Man uses 6,000,000 square miles.

Fields of Study (ologies) derived from Student Enrollment

Agronomics: Study of productivity of land
Microclimatology: Study of local climates

Student Enrollment

9. What is the birth record of the said, Nation of Islam?
Answer: The said, Nation of Islam has no birth record. It has no beginning nor ending.

10. What is the birth record of said, others than Islam?
Answer: Buddhism is 35,000 years old. Christianity is 551 years old.

Fields of Study (ologies) derived from Student Enrollment

Soteriology: Study of theological salvation
Theology: Study of religion; religious doctrine
Patrology: Study of early Christianity

The total list of "ologies" employed in our world today number over 600 sciences, arts and studies of various degrees of respectability and rarity, ranging from the common and esteemed (chemistry) to the

21

obscure and quirky (peristerophily). Over the past century, the range and scope of scientific endeavors has expanded exponentially, so that practically any field of study has a name associated with it. Most of these terms end in 'ology', from the Greek logos, meaning 'word'.

Both Bible and Quran also contain ologies that wise men have learned to put into practice. These ologies were also written in esoteric language too. For example: The in Bible book of Leviticus 17:11, reads: *"For the life of the flesh is in the blood, and I have given it to you upon the altar to make atonement for your souls; for it is the blood that makes atonement for the soul."* What is the esoteric message here? Of course, it is human physiology! In 1616, William Harvey discovered that blood circulation is the key factor in physical life—confirming what the Bible revealed 3,000 years earlier. He found that blood carries water and nourishment to every cell, maintains the body's temperature, and removes the waste material of the body's cells. The blood also carries oxygen from the lungs throughout the body.[8]

On the other hand, the Holy Quran says in Chapter 96:15-16: *"Let him beware! If he does not stop, We will take him by the Naseyah (front of the head), a lying, sinful Naseyah (from of the head)."* Why did the Quran describe the front of the head as being lying and sinful? Why didn't the Quran say that the person was lying and sinful? What is the relationship between the front of the head and lying and sinfulness? If we look into the skull at the front of the head, we will find the prefrontal area of the

---

[8] The DEFENDER'S Study Bible, Word Publishing, Grand Rapids, Michigan (1995).

22

cerebrum, in the area we call the forehead. What does *physiology* tell us about the function of this area?

A book entitled Essentials of Anatomy & Physiology says about this area, "The motivation and the foresight to plan and initiate movements occur in the anterior portion of frontal lobes, the prefrontal area. This is a region of association cortex. Also the book says, 'In relation to its involvement in planning, motivating, and initiating good and sinful behavior, and is responsible for the telling of lies and the speaking of truth. So, it is proper for the telling of lies and the speaking of truth. So, it is proper to describe the front of the head as lying and sinful when someone lies or commits a sin, as the Quran says: '...*A lying, sinful Naseyah (from of the head)*."

Scientists have only discovered these functions of the prefrontal area in the last sixty years, according to Professor Keith L. Moore author of Scientific Miracles in the Front of the Head p. 41.

Nation of Islam Decoded: Sciences of Mankind will further make manifest the ideas derived from the ologies (field of study) of the Supreme Wisdom Book whose esoteric language is like the epistemological models of the scriptures' of Gods prophets. No nation of people on earth can flourish without producing offspring who will master and apply such fields of study called ologies.

Elijah Muhammad's Teacher was truly a friend of America's despised and rejected so-called "Negro" population as they were called during the 1930's. The science of his writing in the Supreme Wisdom Book had its roots in the epistemological model for all the sciences of man. In fact, the F.B.I. seized these lessons after arresting Mr. Elijah Muhammad in 1942 on charges of sedition, conspiracy, and violation of the draft laws. He was accused of sympathizing with the

23

Japanese during World War II and of encouraging his members to resist the military draft. He had, indeed, argued that all nonwhites are oppressed by whites, and that it made no sense for African Americans to fight those who were victims of white racism as much as they themselves were... For his words and actions Muhammad spent four years, from 1942 to 1946, in federal prison at Milan, Michigan.[9]

It is my belief that the F.B.I. and its U.S. intelligence-linguist upon seizing a copy of the secret lessons began decoding every word, the unity of its phonè, glossa, and the logos to see what type of ideological weapon was Elijah given by his Teacher to inspire a "Black Innovative Consciousness." That is to say, the academic linguist knows the concept of writing should define the field of a science, and the science of writing should therefore look for its object at the roots of scientificity.

Every nation needs scientificity represented to its population to govern their consciousness, activity and commerce affairs. As mentioned earlier, the Christian Bible and the Muslim book of scripture, Holy Quran, is complete with scientificity. In fact, its scientificity nourished Europe's consciousness to rise out of the dark ages. It is obvious that her spiritual leaders (Jurist, Popes, Cardinals, Masons, Monks and Elders of Zionism) had the great sense of knowing how to interpret and decode the knowledge shared with them by the ancient[s] of days.

I think the Japanese, Koreans, Chinese and people of modern day India best exemplify how "third" world nations become "first" world nations. All of them have prepared men and women of science who have

---

[9] www.africawithin.com/bios/elijah_muhammad.htm

24

mastered, to some degree, the sciences of life, commerce, trade, industry—i.e. ologies. Black Americans can't get mad. They must get busy! (smile)

Chapter 3

Lost Found Muslim Lesson No. 1

Lost Found Muslim Lesson No. 1 contain 22 questions written by W. Fard Muhammad—the Finder of the Lost and Found members of the Nation of Islam in North America. Some of the early pioneers of the N.O.I. who saw and heard him teach were interviewed by Nathaniel 10X during the 1970's. It is interesting to read what one old pioneer by the name of Frank X had to say:

> *"TIMES WERE NOT EASY in those days and Muslims were few, and they were not loved by Lost-Found nor white. 'Many times when the landlord found out that you were Muslim, you had to get out.' Brother Frank X remembers. There were also many other trials and hardships. These were depression years, hostile years. There were many responsibilities, and many posts to command.*
>
> *"Brother Frank X's recollections capture the jubilance and joy and happiness that Master Fard Muhammad showed when he was among the believers. 'He was always happy,' Bro. Frank said. 'He would come in bowing. He would say, 'It's been a long time since I've seen my uncle (so-called Negro). I promised Abraham that I'd come after you. I told Abraham I'd go and gather them myself, I won't send anyone, I'll go myself'. When Brother Frank first heard the teaching in early 1933, these were depression years and times were hard."*[10]

---

[10] Story and Photos By Nathaniel 10X, Muhammad Speaks Newspaper

Before I present the ologies of Lesson No. 1, consider the biblical passage of Genesis 9:25, *"Cursed be Canaan; a servant of servants shall he be unto his brethren."* After reading Noah's Curse: The Biblical Justification of American Slavery by Stephen R. Haynes you may come to see why old European religious institutions *once* brainwashed the world to believe blacks, dark skinned people or Africans were predestined slaves. Of course, the misunderstood ologies derived from *Genesis 9:25* encouraged Europe and America to form an abominable business called the Atlantic Slave Trade.

However, to learn "a root knowledge" how and why the Western world accepted legal slavery and systemized suppression of black skinned people, pay attention to the ologies (field of studies) of Lost Found Muslim Lesson No. 1. They were what the early founding pioneers read, studied and memorized. These particular lessons make known many subjects spoken publicly and secretly by ancient Egyptians, Greeks and Romans who spoke of them as myths. The institutions that govern such subjects were formed in religion and military stratagem.

Lost Found Muslim Lesson No. 1

1. Why isn't the devil settled on the best part of the planet Earth?
ANS:- Because the earth belongs to the original black man. And knowing that the devil was wicked and there would not be any peace among them, he put him out in the worst part of the earth and kept the best part preserved for himself ever since he made it. The best part is in Arabia at the Holy City Mecca. The colored man or Caucasian is the devil…

Fields of Study (ologies) derived from
Lost Found Muslim Lesson No. 1

Ctetology; Study of the inheritance of acquired characteristics
Pychognosy: Study of mentality; personality or character
Polemology: Study of War
Etymology: Study of origins of words
Demology: Study of human behaviour

Lost Found Muslim Lesson No. 1

4. Why did we run Yacob and his made devil from the root of civilization, over the hot desert, into the cave of West Asia, as they now call it, Europe? What is the meaning of Eu and Rope? How long ago? What did the devil bring with him? What kind of life did he live? And how long before Mossa came to teach the devil of the forgotten tricknollegy?

Fields of Study (ologies) derived from
Lost Found Muslim Lesson No. 1

Hamartiology: Study of sin
Irenology: The study of peace
Sociobiology: Study of study of biological basis of human behaviour
Characterology: Study of development of character

Lost Found Muslim Lesson No. 1

12. What is the meaning of F.O.I.?
ANS.-The Fruit of Islam; the name given to the military training of the men that belong to Islam in North America.

13. What is the meaning of Lieu. and Capt.?
ANS.-Captain and Lieutenant. The duty of a captain is to give orders to the lieutenant, and the lieutenant's duty is to teach the private soldiers; also train them.

14. What is the meaning of M.G.T. and G.C.C?
ANS.-Muslim Girls' Training and General Civilization Class. This was the name given to the training of women and girls in North America; how to keep house, how to rear children, how to take care of their husbands, sew, cook, and, in general, how to act at home and abroad. ...

Fields of Study (ologies) derived from Lost Found Muslim Lesson No. 1

Stratography: Art of leading an army
Polemology: Study of war
Aretaics: The science of virtue
Hygiatics: Study of development of character
Magirics: Art of cookery
Neonatology: Study of newborn babies
Oikology: Science of housekeeping
Paedology: Study of Children
Paedotrophy: Art of rearing children
Sexology: Study of sexual behaviour
Proxemics: Study of man's need for personal space

Lost Found Muslim Lesson No. 2

Lost Found Muslim Lesson No. 2 is the fifth lesson of the Supreme Wisdom Book. It contains 40 questions. Mr. Elijah Muhammad answered these questions posed to him by his Master Teacher, Wallace Fard Muhammad. The lesson text begin as follows:

> *"This LESSON is ANSWERED Very Near Correct and ALL STUDENTS should READ AND STUDY it until he or she can RECITE it by HEART."*
>
> Prophet, W.D. Fard

FIRST TERM EXAMINATION
ASSIGNMENT
of
Mr. Elijah Muhammad

Elijah Muhammad responded to this particular lesson in 1934. Notice in the quote below where he referred to his Teacher as Prophet, W. D. Fard:

"This Lesson No. 2 was given by our Prophet, W. D. Fard which contains 40 questions answered by Elijah Muhammad, one of the Lost-Founds in the wilderness of North America February 20th, 1934."

One of the keys here is the year in which Elijah Muhammad signed this lesson. It is my belief he not only understood the esoteric meaning behind the Supreme Wisdom Book, he also fully understood how to apply them. His limitations; however, were the number of qualified black men and women of science he needed to help him. Nevertheless, in spite of discriminatory laws against Black Americans by the U.S. Government, he and the early pioneers of the N.O.I. from 1934 to 1975 established:

- Muhammad's Temples in every city in America as well as in Jamaica, the British Honduras and England
- Over 46 Muhammad Universities of Islam in America
- Thousands of acres of farmland in Georgia, Michigan, Alabama and other states including dairy farms and a 50 acre apple orchard
- Low rent apartment complexes in Chicago for over 800 people
- The Guaranty Bank and Trust Company (a Black bank!)
- Your Supermarket grocery stores
- Salaam restaurants, Shabazz Bakeries, Capitol Dry Cleaners
- Temple no.2 Clothing store, Muslim Import Store
- Chicago Lamb Packers, Food processing canning factory
- Shabazz Barber shops, Salaam Snack shop

- Progressive Land Development
- A fixed aviation department in Gary, Indiana with our own plane
- The Muslim Fish program (at its peak 3 million tons a month of whiting H&G fish from Peru and Chile
- A fleet of cross-country tractor trailer trucks for transportation of goods and merchandise
- The Muhammad Speaks newspaper, which at its peak sold close to one million copies every issue

By 1975 the Honorable Elijah Muhammad presided over a Black enterprise worth an estimated 85 million dollars. By today's standard, that is Billions. For his great work among his people, Mayor Richard Daley proclaimed *March 29* **"The Honorable Elijah Muhammad Day."**

Holidays set aside to Honor The Messenger On March 27, 1974, at a time when it was extremely unpopular for public officials to openly laud the achievements of the Nation of Islam, MAYOR RICHARD DALEY, who served as Mayor of Chicago, Illinois for 21 years (from 1955 until his death in 1976), issued a proclamation declaring March 29, as the Honorable Elijah Muhammad Day in Chicago that read:

"WHEREAS, on the evening of Friday, March 29, 1974, a citizens' committee will hold a testimonial dinner at the Conrad Hotel to the Honorable Elijah Muhammad; and

"WHEREAS, mutual respect and brotherhood are essential for people to live in harmony everywhere; and

"WHEREAS, the Honorable Elijah Muhammad has exhibited strong leadership to provide quality education, to establish prosperous business, to organize recreational activities and to develop good citizenship in the community; and

"WHEREAS, the proceeds from this testimonial dinner will be used to support the construction of a 300 bed hospital on the South Side:

NOW, THEREFORE, I, Richard J. Daley, Mayor of the City of Chicago, do hereby proclaim March 29, 1974 to be HONORABLE ELIJAH MUHAMMAD DAY IN CHICAGO and call upon all citizens to take cognizance of the special events arranged for this time."

Dated this 27th day of March, 1974
Richard J. Daley, Mayor

Thus far, The Supreme Wisdom Book written by Master Wallace Fard Muhammad proves both scientific and philosophical. It's influence upon the Honorable Elijah Muhammad and his followers activated them to lay the elements of nationhood three decades before Jim Crow was outlawed. The lesson books "englobes of Divine Wisdom in the Adamic Word" reflect what thousands of Muslim peripatetic's were attempting to write centuries ago in Indo-European languages to express universal principles and sciences of the ancients. However, the righteous man from the east, Master Wallace Fard Muhammad, did it in 6 sets of lessons in 154 questions and answers.

Lost Found Muslim Lesson No. 2

1. Who made the Holy Koran or Bible?
How long ago? Will you tell us why does Islam re-new her history every twenty-five thousand years?

2. What makes rain, hail, snow and earthquakes?

33

Fields of Study (ologies) derived from Lost Found Muslim Lesson No. 2

Codicology: Study of manuscripts
Pisteology: Science of study of faith
Soteriology: Study of theological salvation
Historiography: Study of writing history
Crypotology: Study of codes
Climatology: Study of climate
Hydrometeorology: Study of atmospheric moisture
Hyetology: Science of rainfall
Hygrology: Study of humidity
Meteorology: Study weather
Nephology: Study of clouds
Astrometeorolgy: Study of effect of stars on climate
Seismology: Study of earthquakes
Stratigraphy: Study of geological layers or strata

Lost Found Muslim Lesson No. 2

9. Why does the devil teach the eighty-five percent that a mystery God brings all this?
ANS – To conceal the true God, which is the Son of man, and make slaves out of the 85% by keeping them worshipping something he knows they cannot see (invisible), and he lives and makes himself rich from their labor. The 85% know that it rains, hails and snows; also, hear it thunder above his head, but they do not try to learn who is it that causes all of this to happen by letting the 5% teach them. He believes in the 10% on face value.

Fields of Study (ologies) derived from Lost Found Muslim Lesson No. 2

Brontology: Science study of thunder
Electrostatics: Study of static electricity

Lost Found Muslim Lesson No. 2

14. Who is the 85%?
ANS – The uncivilized people; poison animal eaters; slaves from mental death and power; people who do not know the living God or their origin in this world, and they worship that they know not what – who are easily led in the wrong direction, but hard to lead into the right direction.

15. Who is the 10%?
ANS – The rich; the slave-makers of the poor, who teach the poor lies – to believe that the almighty, true and living God is a spook and cannot be seen by the physical eye. Otherwise known as the blood-sucker of the poor.

Fields of Study (ologies) derived from Lost Found Muslim Lesson No. 2

Archelogy: The study of first principles
Genealogy: Study of descent of families
Pseudology: Art or science of lying

Lost Found Muslim Lesson No. 2

30. Tell us what and how the devil is made?
ANS – The devil is made from the original people by grafting (separating the germs)…

In the black man, there exists two germs: one a Black germ, and one – a brown germ. Yacob, with his law on birth control, separated the brown germs from the black man and grafted it into a white by destroying the black germ. After following this process for six hundred years, the germ became white, and weak and was no more original. And by thinning the original blood, it became weak, and wicked, and it is no more the same. Thus, this is the way Yacob made the devil.

Fields of Study (ologies) derived from Lost Found Muslim Lesson No. 2

Spermology: Study of seeds
Hematology: Study of blood

Lost Found Muslim Lesson No. 2

38. Then why did God make devil?
ANS – To show for his power, that he is all wise and righteous. That he could make a devil, which is weak and wicked, and give the devil power to rule the Earth for six thousand years and, then destroy the devil in one day without falling a victim to the devil's civilization. Otherwise to show and prove that Allah is the God, always has been and always will be.

Fields of Study (ologies) derived from Lost Found Muslim Lesson No. 2

Deontology: The theory or study of moral obligation

Chapter 4

The Problem Book

The Problem Book is the fifth lesson written by Wallace Fard Muhammad (a.k.a. W. D. Fard). He completed this lesson by employing over 27,686 words, letters and numbers. One interesting aspect about the Problem referred to as "Problem No. 13" of the Problem is that it is the only lesson paragraph mentioned twice within the entire text of the Supreme Wisdom Book. The ologies derived from this particular problem will be provided later. But it reads:

> *"After learning Mathematics, which is Islam, and Islam is Mathematics, it stands true. You can always prove it at no limit of time. Then you must learn to use it and secure some benefit while you are living, that is - luxury, money, good homes, friendship in all walks of life."*

Mr. Elijah Muhammad wrote the Problem Book preamble using the following words:

> *"This book teaches the Lost Found Nation of Islam a through knowledge of our miserable state of condition in a mathematical way when we were found by our Saviour, W.D. Fard".*

You will derive from these secret lesson plans, the ologies (field of studies) that support the nature and solution to resolve what W. D. Fard describe as Problems. Chiefly problems that ill affected the miserable state of Black America during the 1930's and up till this present day. It will also give you an idea about the many fields of science and commerce that a nation of people must engage and apply if they are desirous to become a global intranational powerhouse.

Regrettably, far too many young Black Americans, youth in general, both male and female, continue to go astray to sport and play, *feeble minded for style,* seeking escapism without having fruitful skills to fulfill their wants and desires. Nevertheless, it is never too late. All must maximize one way or another, the fields of study demonstrated heretofore. It must be fulfilled generation after generation after generation. We all understand nothing happens overnight except a one nightstand.

So now let us begin to decipher some fundamental problems and solutions contained in the Problem Book.

Problem Book

1. The uncle of Mr. W.D. Fard lived in the wilderness of North America and he lived other than his own self, therefore, his pulse beat seventy-eight times per minute and this killed him in forty-five years of age. How many times did his pulse beat in forty-five years?

2. The wife of Mr. W.D. Fard's uncle, in the wilderness of North America, weighs other than herself, therefore, she has rheumatism, headaches, pain in all joints, and cannot walk up to the store. She is troubled frequently with high Blood pressure and registers more thirty-two. Her pulse is nearly eighty times per minute and she died at the age of forty-seven. How many times did her pulse beat in forty-seven years?

3. A Sheep contains fourteen square feet. One-tenth of a square inch contains fourteen thousand hairs. How many will the fourteen square feet contain?

4. One one-hundredth of a cubic inches contain two hundred million Atoms. How many will fifty square miles contain?

5. The uncle of Mr. W.D. Fard lives in the wilderness of North America and he is living other than himself, therefore, he weighs more than his height and his blood pressure registers more than thirty-two. This killed him at the age of forty-four years....

6. The second uncle of Mr. W.D. Fard, in the wilderness of North America, lived other than himself and, therefore, his blood pressure registered over thirty-two. He had fever, headaches, chills, grippe, hay fever, regular fever, rheumatism; also pain in all joints. He was disturbed with foot ailments and toothaches....

If the air value selling price, then the third uncle of Mr. W.D. Fard would have been robbed of the Atmosphere. How much air did he breathe more than the average man? Each cubic foot of air costs $10.50.

How much does Mr. W.D. Fard's second uncle robbed in forty-six years? Twenty pills cost twenty-five cents. How much does this amount to in forty-six years?

Fields of Study *(ologies)* derived from *Problem Book*

Sphygmology: Study of the pulse
Symptomoatology: Study of symptoms of illness
Arthrology: Study of joints
Aceology: Therapeutics
Angiology: Study of blood flow and lymphatic system
Cardiology: Study of the heat
Desmology: Study of ligaments
Zoonomy: Animal physiology
Stoichiology: Science of elements of animal tissues
Trichology: Study of hair and its disorders
Somatology: Science of the properties of matter

Threpsology: Science of nutrition
Trophology: Study of nutrition
Odontology: Study of teeth
Virology: Study of viruses
Periodontics: Study of gums
Pyretology: Study fevers
Rheumatology: Study of rheumatism
Palynology: Study of pollen
Osteology: Study of parasites
Podology: Study of feet
Koniology: Study of atmospheric pollutants and dust
Pharmacology: Study of drugs
Posology: Science of quantity of dosage
Acology: Study of medical remedies
Anaesthesiology: Study of anaesthetics

The wealth of professions and industries derived from the aforementioned ologies are as follows under the title of Healthcare:

Dental Laboratories
General Medical and Surgical Hospitals
Health and Allied Services
Home Health Care Services
Intermediate Care Facilities
Kidney Dialysis Centers
Medical Laboratories
Nursing and Personal Care Facilities
Offices and Clinics of Chiropractors
Offices and Clinics of Dentists
Offices and Clinics of Doctors of Medicine
Offices and Clinics of Doctors of Osteopathy
Offices and Clinics of Health Practitioners
Offices and Clinics of Optometrists
Offices and Clinics of Podiatrists
Skilled Nursing Care Facilities,
Specialty Hospitals
Psychiatric Specialty Outpatient Facilities

Problem Book

7. If one one-hundred of a cubic of a inch contains two hundred million atoms, the total Atmosphere weighs eleven and two-thirds quintillion pounds. One-third of eleven and two thirds quintillion pounds equal atoms. Mr. Muhammad cracked one atom into ten million parts. Then Mr. Sharrieff wants to know what will be the weight of the cracked Atom? $100.00 (In Gold) For The Person Who Works This Problem (Qualified Muslims)

Fields of Study (ologies) derived from Problem Book

Aerology: Study of the atmosphere
Physics: Study of properties of matter and energy
Metallogeny: Study of the origin and distribution of metal deposits
Metallography: Study of the structure and constitution of metals
Chrysology: Study of precious metals
Numismatics: Study of currency and its history

Problem Book

9. The population of Detroit is one million five hundred thousand people, and there are two hundred and fifty thousand original nation. During these hard times for the lack of jobs, not having enough money to buy food, they eat two meals per day…

It is also known to the civilized world that ten ounces of the poison animal destroys three one-hundredths percent of the beauty appearance of a person. Then Mr. Muhammad wants to know how long will it take to destroy the whole one hundred percent of the beauty appearance at the above eating rates?

Fields of Study (ologies) derived from Problem Book

Proaxeology: Study of practical or efficient activity; science of efficient action
Eutherics: Science concerned with improving living conditions
Dermatology: Study of skin
Kalology: Study of beauty

Problem Book

11. The Suez Canal in Egypt is ninety miles long, with a depth of thirty-three feet, and a width of one hundred twenty-two feet. The cost to build it sixty-four years ago was one hundred fifty million dollars. Mr. A. Ali has five hundred dollars worth of stock in it at the rate of six and three-fifths percent. Now he wants to know how much money he has coming to him at the above rate from 1869 to May 26, 1933...

Fields of Study (ologies) derived from Problem Book

Notaphily: Collecting of bank-notes and cheques
Catalactics: Science of commercial exchange

In Problem 11, the following business opportunities may be derived from some of its words and ideas, e.g. Business Services & Administration, Diversified Services, Financial Services, Insurance and Legal Services, Professional Services, Real Estate Services, Banks and other companies that generate profit through investment and management of capital.

Problem Book

12. The Area of the Planet is one hundred ninety-six million, nine hundred forty thousand square miles and she weighs six sextillion tons. Mr. Shah wants to know how much does the State of Michigan weigh? Going by the Book Of

42

Darkness – saying that the State of Michigan is fifty-seven thousand, nine hundred eighty square miles and has a population of four million, eight hundred forty-two thousand, two hundred eighty people…

One cubic foot of common Earth weighs eighty pounds. One common Ca. weighs one hundred seventy pounds. The average original weighs one hundred fifty pounds and there are five hundred thousand original nations living in the State of Michigan; approximately eight million live stock of all kinds….

Don't tell her that there was no one to teach you for three hundred and seventy -nine years. She already knows and is trying to forget it. Now she will teach you quickly any course you may desire.

Fields of Study (ologies) derived from Problem Book

Geography: Study of surface of the earth and its inhabitants
Zoopathology: Study of animal diseases
Zoogeography: Study of geographic distribution of animals
Zootechnics: Science of breeding animals
Rhochrematics: Science of inventory management and the movement of products

Earlier I mentioned how Problem 13 is written twice. Following this stated problem below are its sciences that if implemented, secures any nation from poverty and want.

Problem Book

13. After learning Mathematics, which is Islam, and Islam is Mathematics, it stands true. You can always prove it at no limit of time. Then you must learn to use it and secure some benefit while you are living – that is luxury, money, good homes, friendships in all walks of life….

Now you must speak the Language so you can use your mathematical Theology in the proper term, otherwise you will not be successful...

There are twenty-six letters in the Language and if a Student Learns one letter per day, then how long will it take him to learn the twenty-six letters?

There are ten numbers in the Mathematic Language. Then how long will it take a Student to learn the whole ten numbers (at the above rate?)

Fields of Study (ologies) derived from Problem Book

Mathematics: Study of magnitude, number, and forms
Ecomonics: Study of material wealth
Chrematistics: The study of wealth; political economy
Tonetics: Study of pronunciation
Phoniatrics: Study and correction of speech defects
Phonology: Study of speech sounds
Orthography: Study of spelling
Numerology: Study of numbers

Problem Book

14. The University of Al-Azhar, in Cairo, has a Student population of thirty-six hundred; all but one-tenth taking other than language, three-tenths taking Construction Engineering, two-tenths taking Civil Engineering, three-tenths taking Mechanical Engineering, and the rest taking Teachership.

Fields of Study (ologies) derived from Problem Book

Egyptology: Study of ancient Egypt
Electrology: Study of electricity
Ichnography: Art of drawing ground plans
Glossology: Study of language; study of the tongue
Lexicology: Study of words and their meanings
Lexigraphy: Art of definition of words

Linguistics: Study of language
Ideogeny: Study of origins of ideas
Orthoepy: Study of correct pronunciation
Syntax: Study of sentence structure

On the matter of Engineering shown in Problem 14, the Honorable Elijah Muhammad responded to the necessity of this science among Black people in a letter he wrote to one of his followers on August 6, 1968.[11]

The Honorable Elijah Muhammad
Messenger of Allah
4847 South Woodlawn Avenue
Chicago, Illinois 60615
August 6, 1968

As-Salaam-Alaikum

In the Name of Almighty Allah, The Most Merciful Saviour, our Deliverer, who Came in the Person of Master Fard Muhammad, to whom praises are due forever, Master of the day of Judgment. To Allah alone do I submit and seek refuge.

Dear Brother:

I was so happy reading your letter dated July 10, 1968 of your contributions to the cause of Islam. I pray Allah will reward you so that you will not have any want for material things of this world.

Regarding your education and striving towards an Engineers degree, **you have to get the knowledge from those that know.** If you want to work part of the

---

[11] http://www.muhammadspeaks.com/lettertomuhammadzahir.html

time, and go to school part of the day, and you cannot arrange it differently, I say take it. If you are able to school yourself without trying to work at the same time on some job, I would look into that; because, **education is what the so-called Negro needs**.

At the proper time we will need to know all types of Engineering. We have to re-build for ourselves the type of Civilization that Allah demands us to accept. **In words to say--we have to rebuild a Nation. Engineering is the first trade that will be in demand.**

Thank you, may Allah bless you, and if there is anything the Nation can aid you in, feel not ashamed to ask any advice that you think is in us. Please do not hesitate in seeking the answer.

As-Salaam-Alaikum
Elijah Muhammad
Messenger of Allah
EM/vn/b2x

So far in the Problem Book I believe the signs pointing to how a nation of people evolve is obvious. Below you see more industries, institutions and businesses that may derive from the ideas contained in lessons 13 and 14. But who wants to study and endure the *demanding* process of learning how to fulfill them?

Service Industries
Educational Services
Media Production
Printing/Publishing
Transportation
Warehousing & Storage

Industrial Markets
Advanced Materials
Aerospace & Defense
Automotive/Transportation & Shipping
Electrical & Electronics
Energy & Resources

Environmental Markets
Fabrication
Manufacturing &
Construction
Materials & Chemicals
Subassemblies/
Instruments

Public Sector
Associations/Non-Profits
Defense
Government
Housing

Educational Services

Books, Periodicals, and
Newspapers
Business and Secretarial
Schools
Colleges, Universities,
and Professional Schools
Data Processing Schools
Elementary and
Secondary Schools
Junior Colleges and
Technical Institutes
Libraries
Schools and Educational
Services,
Vocational Schools, NEC

Problem Book

17. Mars, the inhabited Planet, is one hundred forty-one million, five hundred thousand miles from the Sun, and she travels one thousand thirty-seven and one-third miles per hour. Her diameter is four thousand two hundred miles.

18. Mercury is also an inhabited Planet and is thirty-six million miles from the Sun. Her diameter is three thousand miles…

24. Platoon is four billion, six hundred million miles from the Sun and she travels the same rate around the Sun as the rest of the Planets. It takes her three hundred forty-five years to make on complete circle around the Sun…
25. What is the Physical Standard of a devil against the original.

How many ounces of brain does an Original have?

27. The Universe Diameter equals seventy-six quintillion miles. What is the Area in Square miles. What is the Area in Square Yards? Give your answer in Figures only.

Fields of Study (ologies) derived from Problem Book

Areology: Study of Mars
Planetology: Study of planets
Astrogeology: Study of extraterrestial geology
Uranology: Study of the heavens; astronomy
Astronomy: Study of celestial bodies
Astrophysics: Study of behaviour of interstellar matter
Astroseimology: Study of star oscillations
Uranography: Descriptive astronomy and mapping
Statics: Study of bodies and forces in equilibrium
Anthropobiology: Study of human biology
Cosmology: Study of the universe

Life on Mars and other planets

Obviously the above series of Supreme Wisdom Book lessons open the mind to astronomy—the scientific study of the universe, especially of the motions, positions, sizes, composition, and behavior of astronomical objects. Before going into the industrial and employment derivatives of astronomy, let us read what Elijah Muhammad taught the early pioneers of the Nation of Islam during a 1960 speech in Baltimore, Maryland:

> *"And God Almighty has revealed the secret to me and not only the secret of the moon and the earth to me, but has also given to me the secret knowledge of more planets, other than the earth, even to Mars, the civilization on it and they have the language of the people on Mars and they can speak to these people, they can question them. They can make them react to our will. But they cannot make us react to their will.*

48

"They are a people that is not exactly like us, but they walk on two feet, like you and I. But they are taller than we are. And they are more skinnier than we are. And they live 1,200 of our earth years. The white race have been suspecting that there was life on Mars, not only on Mars but there is life on Venus.

"There is life on many of the other planets. Seven planets of our Solar System have life on it. And it is known. But it is not known to the white world because they are a very young people, who were just brought about in the last 6,000 years and their science, their knowledge of astronomy just came about here less than 500 years ago. And the old original astronomy among our people who today, keeps his mouth shut, in order that he may not enrich the present world with such knowledge, they have kept it as a secret.

But today, as it is written, the secret of God and the universe must be made known because it is the last days of this world". [12]

You ask: what is the purpose of astronomy? Astronomy plays a much more practical role that is not nearly as important today as it was in the past. Since the time of our earliest ancestors, humans have used the motions of celestial objects to position themselves in space and time.

During the Renaissance, advances in mathematics coupled with the invention of new observational instruments (like the refracting telescope) gave rise to modern astronomy. Studies into the force of gravity led to the creation of celestial mechanics: a new branch of astronomy that allowed the motions of astronomical objects to be

---

[12] www.muhammadspeaks.com/Baltimore1960.html

49

mathematically predicted for the first time ever. Astrometry and celestial mechanics became the two main fields of study for astronomers, whereas astrology was relegated to the status of pseudo-science and no longer practiced by astronomers.

From the 19th century onwards, the discovery of the electromagnetic spectrum and the world of the atom spurred on the development of astrophysics, a new discipline in astronomy that is now considered to be the most important.[13]

Case in point, astronomy and physics classes may require a two-year cycle of 13, one-quarter courses.

Six courses are specifically required:
Astonomy 202, Electromagnetism and Plasma Physics
Astonomy 204A, Physics of Astrophysics I
Astonomy 204B, Physics of Astrophysics II
Astonomy 205, Introduction to Astronomical Research
Astonomy 220A, Stella Structure and Evolution
Astonomy 240A, Galactic and Extragalactic Stellar Systems

Seven courses are chosen from the list of electives given below. Students must meet at least quarterly with an assigned adviser. Each student must also be a teaching assistant for at least one quarter. By the end of their second year, students must complete one quarter of independent study with a faculty member and give a department talk on that work. After passing a board review based on the above-mentioned requirements and a qualifying exam based on a proposed thesis topic (expected to be taken before the end of the third year), students pursue independent research leading to the doctoral dissertation.

---

[13] astro-canada.ca/_en/a1102.html

Upon completion of the Ph.D. dissertation, students must pass an oral dissertation defense. Students are encouraged to engage in research projects under the supervision of the faculty during the early part of their graduate career. Exceptions are rare and are granted on a case-by-case basis to individual students. Electives may be drawn from this list:

Galaxies and Cosmology (at least two):
Astonomy 214, Structure Formation in the Universe
Astonomy 224, Origin and Evolution of the Universe
Astonomy 230, Low-Density Astrophysics
Astonomy 233, Physical Cosmology
Astonomy 240B, Galactic and Extragalactic Stellar Systems
Astonomy 240C, Galactic and Extragalactic Stellar Systems
Astonomy 253, Stellar Dynamics

Stars and Planets (at least two):
Astonomy 212, Dynamical Astronomy
Astonomy 220B, Star and Planet Formation
Astonomy 220C, Advanced Stages of Stellar Evolution and Nucleosynthesis
Astonomy 222, Planetary Science
Astonomy 225, Physics of Compact Objects
Astonomy 237, Accretion of Early and Late Stages of Stellar Evolution

Other:
Astonomy 207, Future Directions/Future Missions
Astonomy 226, General Relativity
Astonomy 231, Astrophysical Gas Dynamics
Astonomy 235, Numerical Techniques
Astonomy 257, Modern Observational Techniques
Astonomy 260, Instrumentation for Astronomy
Astonomy 275, Radio Astronomy
Astonomy 289C, Adaptive Optics and Its Applications
Earth Sciences 275, Magnetohydrodynamics
Education 286, Research and Practice in Science Training

for Research

Engineering 206, Bayesian Statistics
Physics 210, Classical Mechanics
Physics 215, Introduction to Non-Relativistic Quantum Mechanics
Physics 216, Advanced Topics in Non-Relativistic Quantum Mechanics
Physics 217, Quantum Field Theory I
Physics 218, Quantum Field Theory II

Not everyone will go on to work as an astrophysicists but your training will open the door to a whole range of other exciting and challenging careers. As a physicist a lot of job opportunities will be open to you. Astrophysics courses are designed to enable you to develop skills in a number of areas useful for a career in science.

For example you will develop skills in problem solving and working together in a team. You will also learn many other things useful for a career in physics. Furthermore, you will learn about instrumentation, lasers, digital image processing, basic electronics and computer software development.

As a physicist, job prospects are good. Fields where you are likely to be employed as a physicist are:

Renewable energy (an increasingly important field)
Communications
Opto-electronics (lasers etc)
Materials science
Instrumentation (electronic measuring equipment)
Testing, Teaching
Medicine (eg. as a medical physicist)
Information Technology

Many government and industrial research laboratories and hospitals etc., employ physicists.[14] But who wants to study and endure the *demanding* process of learning how to fulfill the task?

Problem Book

30. The uncle of Mr. W.D. Fard lives in the wilderness of North America, surrounded and robbed completely by the Cave man. Therefore, he has no knowledge of his own nor anyone else's, but his mind travels twenty-four billion miles per second, which is considered the average speed of thought per second.

How many round trips will he make in ten seconds to the far Planet Platoon?

Fields of Study (ologies) derived from Problem Book

Victimology: Study of victims
Nomology: The science of the laws; especially of the mind
Metaphysics: Study of principles of nature and thought
Metapsychology: Study of nature of mind
Psychobiology: Study of biology of the mind
Psychology: Study of mind
Psychophysics: Study of link between mental and physical processes

Lesson 30 of the Problem Book is clearly a subject about the human mind or neuroscience. Is neuroscience science important for a nation to understand and to take advantage of?

In South Korea, an invited gathering of many of the world's top neuroscientists met. The event was held at the uber futuristic W hotel convention center and open to the public. And they came, by the

---

[14] astrophysics.qut.edu.au/careers_for_physicists.asp

thousands families with kids, high schoolers, professionals, other scientists. South Korea is a place where scientists are treated with the enthusiasm most Americans only give to some talent less celebrities or rap star. Newly-elected South Korea President, Lee Myung-bak, spoke at the opening ceremony and reminded the audience his country now has the tenth strongest economy in the world. Ninety percent of all Korean kids go on to college....He also recalled that he comes from the world of business and entrepreneurialism -- and he's determined that his country will be a leader in neuroscience and related technologies.[15]

Problem Book

31. A lion in a cage walks back and forth, sixty feet per minute, seeking a way out of the cage. It took nearly four centuries to find the door. Now, with modern equipment, he is walking three thousand feet per minute and he has three thousand miles by two thousand miles to go yet. How long will it take him to cover this territory of said, three thousand by two thousand miles, at the above walking rate? Five thousand two hundred eight feet equals one mile.

He also has seventeen million keys, which he turns at the rate of sixteen and seventeen one-hundredths per minute. How long will it take him to turn the whole seventeen million? Sixty minutes equal one hour. Twenty-four hours equal one day. Three hundred sixty-five days equal one year.

The above figures do not include rusty locks. It has been said by the labors of Islam, for allowing extra time to oil the rusty locks is sufficient.

---

[15] The New York Times, Saturday, May 10, 2008

Fields of Study (ologies) derived from Problem Book

Technology: The study, development, and application of devices, machines, and techniques for manufacturing and productive processes
Homilectics: The art of preaching

Imagine the commerce derived by modern equipment and other means of mass communication media to free the masses from intense manual labor, bondage and spiritual ignorance.

Machine Technology	Information Technology
Media	Markets/Demographics
Wireless	Media Satellite
Computer Hardware	Communication
Networking	Software & Enterprise
E-Commerce	Computing
IT Outsourcing	

All of the above fields of study and innovations are being employed in our world today. Western world men and women dominate the brains and money behind the development and management of these operations. I reiterate, can Black America engage and excel; can Africa engage and excel? Of course they can!

Problem Book

32. Twelve Leaders of Islam from all over the Planet have conferred in the Root of Civilization concerning the Lost Found Nation of Islam; must return to their original Land.

One of the Conference Members, by the name of Mr. Osman Sharrieff, said to the eleven Members of the Conference: "The Lost Found Nation of Islam will not return to their original land unless they, first, have a thorough knowledge of their own". So they sent a Messenger to them of their own.

Now, the Messenger and his Labors worked day and night for the last three and one-half years, and their accomplishment is approximately twenty-five thousand. The Messenger and his Labors are worried, for the time of Laboring is mentioned and limited in said, Problem No.

31. One of the Prophets in the early days said: "The Lost Found Nation of Islam numbering one hundred forty-four thousand, will be Stars, and will return to their original Land. And the Balance", he said, "are poison and rusty, and will not take the Knowledge of their own".

But the Messenger and his Labors do not agree with the old Prophets in this modern time…

Fields of Study (ologies) derived from Problem Book

Metapolitics: Study of politics in theory or abstract
Stasiology: Study of political parties
Ergology: Study of effects of work on humans
Psychoacoustics: Recovery of messages by brain
Noology: Science of the intellect

Problem Book

33. Lake Michigan is three hundred nine and one-third miles long, sixty-nine and one half miles wide, and she has a depth of eight hundred sixty-eight and one fourth feet. What would be the square mileage of this Cave man's Lake? Reduce to square Yards and inches.

One thousand seven hundred twenty-eight cubic inches equal one cubic foot. One gallon of water contains two hundred thirty-one cubic inches. On cubic foot of water contains seven and one half gallons. One thousand seven hundred twenty-eight cubic inches of water weigh sixty-two and one-half pounds.

Mr. E. Muhammad wants to know if thirteen Ducks – six drink one ounce per day and seven drink three-fourth ounces per day, how long will it take them to dry the Cave Man's Lake? What would be the total weight of water in this Cave man's Lake? Extract the cube root of the total amount of water after having all dry by the thirteen Ducks.

Fields of Study (ologies) derived from Problem Book

Hydrography: Study of investigating bodies of water
Hydrogeology: Study of ground water
Hydrology: Study of water resources
Metrology: Science of weights and measures
Neossology: Study of nestling birds
Ornithology: Study of birds

Problem Book

34. The uncle of Mr. W.D. Fard lives in the wilderness of North America and works sixteen hours out of twenty-four every day for a very little day. He has a large family to support and, on top of that, a Satan came along and sold him Life insurance, and gave him a written Guarantee that he will receive a full benefit at once after approval of his death.

Another Satan came along and sold him five hundred B. Shares at six percent, in the Panama Canal, at $1.75 per Share. The Panama Canal was completed in 1914 at a cost of $375,000,000. Mostly the bigger part of the sum belongs to the Share-Holders, whom we call the 85%.

The Panama Canal is fifty and one-half miles long, three hundred feet wide and has a depth of forty-five feet. What would be the amount of water in weight and gallons belonging to the uncle of Mr. W.D. Fard since there were nine thousand, nine hundred fifty-seven Share-Holders, not including the 15%.

Fields of Study (ologies) derived from Problem Book

Ethonomics: Study of economic and ethical principles of a society
Catalactics: Science of commercial exchange
Cambistry: Science of internatinal exchange
Scripopphily: Collection of bond and share certificates

A more meticulous look at the wealth of ideas derived from the words contained in Problem 34 is as follows:

Financial Services

Branches and Agencies of Foreign Banks
Central Reserve Depository Institutions, NEC
Commercial Banks, NEC
Commodity Contracts Brokers and Dealers
Credit Unions, Federally Chartered
Credit Unions, Not Federally Chartered
Education, Religious, and Charitable Trusts
Federal Reserve Banks
Federal and Federally-Sponsored Credit Agencies
Foreign Trade and International Banking Institutions
Functions Related to Deposit Banking, NEC
Investment Advice
Investors, NEC
Loan Brokers
Management Investment Offices,
Miscellaneous Business Credit Institutions
Mortgage Bankers and Loan Correspondents
National Commercial Banks
Nondeposit Trust Facilities
Offices of Bank Holding Companies
Offices of Holding Companies, NEC
Oil Royalty Traders

Patent Owners and Lessors
Personal Credit Institutions
Real Estate Investment Trusts
Savings Institutions, Federally Chartered
Savings institutions, Not Federally
Chartered
Security Brokers, Dealers, and Flotation Companies
Security and Commodity Exchanges
Services Allied With the Exchange of Securities or
Commodities, NEC
Short-Term Business Credit Institutions, Except Agricultural
State Commercial Banks
Tax Return Preparation Services
Trusts, Except Educational, Religious, and Charitable
Unit Investment Trusts, Face-Amount Certif.

Insurance

Accident and Health Insurance
Fire, Marine, and Casualty Insurance
Hospital and Medical Service Plans
Insurance Agents Brokers, and Service
Insurance Carriers, NEC
Life Insurance
Pension, Health, and Welfare Funds
Surety Insurance
Title Insurance

It is awe-inspiring as one comes to terms with the type of institutions, commerce and trade derived from Problem 34 alone. On the other hand, it may be intimidating to the mentally dead (lazy minded) thinker. Therefore, what is needed now is a user-friendly introduction to these attainable fields of study. The implementation of these fields is the only path to Nationhood. No one, in this day and time, should be held back from accessing a profession that best suits his or her nature to advance their personal and/or national needs!

And so, the superlative textology used in the esoteric language of the Supreme Wisdom Book is undeniable. However, why didn't Wallace Fard Muhammad write straightforwardly what is demonstrated now? Answer: There is no such thing as an illiterate lazy mind Muslim? Besides, three million Caucasian Moslem sons inhabit America who also expected his arrival as it was written in their esoteric scripts too (John 14:9-28). Moreover, some of these types participated in writing the constitution of the 13 Colonies of America, formed the U.S. Supreme Court and supported the first U.S. Public Schools. These Moslem sons (Masons) have been around since mid 1700's. Some are good some are evil minded.[16] But they all secretly acknowledge the True and Living God (Allah) and recognized the scientificity of His writing!

Metaphorical language

The Supreme Wisdom Book of the Nation of Islam in North America contains metaphorical language in the same spirit and soul as all other sacred books. Besides the Bible and the Holy Quran, it also serves as their *religious* text. It has been their coded book since July 4, 1930. So this is one reason why it is said by registerd members of the N.O.I., *"All Praise is Due To Allah, Who came in the Personage of Master Wallace Fard Muhammad."* He is the one who gave them Supreme Wisdom, not Rome, Mecca Israel or the Moslem sons.

Metaphorical language is a term referring to the use of a complex system of metatphors to create a sub-language within a common language which

---

[16] http://www.wncmasons.com/history.htm

provides the basic terms (verbs, prepositions, conjunctions) to express metaphors. This is a common feature of religious discussion, (for example midrash or medieval Roman Catholic "common places" or modern biblespeak) wherein fluency in a religious text is often a prerequisite to participating fully in a conversation. Not just conceptual metaphors (part of every language) that express belief in analogy between generic concepts, but extremely specific metaphors involving proper names or use of concrete nouns to express generics or processes.

The Tao te ching is considered by many to be almost entirely metaphorical. For example, change is usually expressed with the "water" character, not the "change" character. To the outsider, such terms in such combinations will likely seem esoteric or otherwise unintelligible. Only by learning the underlying patterns of events that are considered important in the religion or ethical or political system, would one be able to comprehend what was said. The religious text thus acts as a code book. Since many religious authorities believe in the self-evident truth of their doctrines, a mere exposure to the truth in the book would tend to convert outsiders trying to learn the language. However, use of such language is not confined to religious groups.[17]

I advise you to Google "The Supreme Wisdom". Its language is not confined to a religious group as well.

---

[17] Metaphoric Language from Wikipedia

Chapter 5

English Lesson No. C1

When you read what is called English Lesson No. C1, the concept of "intelligence gathering" comes to mind. Fact is Mr. Elijah Muhammad taught that W. D. Fard who also used the name Wallace Fard Muhammad was in and out of America 20 years—from 1910 to 1930. This also spoke volumes about the data he gathered on America's mistreatment of her former slaves because he witnessed it firsthand, over a 20-year period, without being noticed by white American's due to his "skin color" appearance.

As stated earlier in this book, his mother was a white woman of the caucus mountain range of Eurasia and his father was a jet-black man of Africa. This mixture of black and white gave him the appearance of a white man in the eyes of black and white folk of that era. It was not until he began to publicly teach Black people and gained success among them accepting Islam in the city of Detroit, Michigan and Chicago, Illinois that the F.B.I. set in motion to persecute him in 1932. But, by then it was too late. His best student, Elijah Muhammad, had already accepted the assignment to continue his Teacher's mission—exemplify *intranational* status, build a nation within a nation, inside of America, with Black people, under the rules of Islam.

So what is "intelligence gathering?" Intelligence is not information, but the product of evaluated information, valued for its currency and relevance rather than its detail or accuracy —in contrast with *"data"* which typically refers to *precise or particular* information, or *"fact,"* which typically refers to *verified* information. Sometimes called "active data" or "active intelligence", these typically regard the current plans, decisions, and actions of people, as these may have urgency or may otherwise be considered "valuable" from the point of view of the intelligence-gathering organization. Active intelligence is treated as a constantly mutable component, or variable, within a larger equation of understanding the secret, covert, or otherwise private "intelligence" of an opponent, or competitor, to answer questions or obtain advance warning of events and movements deemed to be important or otherwise relevant.

As used by intelligence agencies and related services, "intelligence" refers integrally to both active data as well as the process and the result of gathering and analyzing such information, as these together form a cohesive network (cf. "hive mind"). In a sense, this usage of "intelligence" at the national level may be somewhat associated with the concept of social intelligence —albeit one which is tied to localized or nationalist tradition, politics, law, and the enforcement thereof.[18]

In short, there are five groups with a relatively permanent "agenda" for any intelligence agency:

- **the President** -- *the ultimate "customer" for which access to determine much of the officeholder's authority and credibility*
- **the Departments -- the State Department**
- **the National Security Council**
- **the Intelligence Community**
- **the Congress**

---

[18] Intelligence (information gathering) from Wikipedia

Every administration should also have a strategic plan, which along with being a classified and secret document is an outline of how, when, and where information on strategic, or long-term, interests and objectives is collected.

As you shall read, English Lesson C1 is truly like reading an intelligence document. It demonstrates how Wallace Fard Muhammad evaluated and analyzed the state of Black America (whom he calls his uncle[19]) after being captured by American Christians for 379 years. (1934 - 379 = 1555)

English Lesson No. C1

1. My name is W. F. Muhammad.[20]
2. I came to North America by myself.
3. My uncle was brought over here by the Trader three hundred seventy-nine years ago.
4. My uncle cannot talk his own language.
5. He does not know that he is my uncle.
6. He likes the devil because the devil gives him nothing.
7. Why does he like the devil?
8. Because the devil put fear in him when he was a little boy.
9. Why does he fear, now since he is a big man?
10. Because the devil taught him to eat the wrong food.
11. Does that have anything to do with the above question, No. 10?
12. Yes sir. That makes him other than his own self.
13. What is his own self?

---

[19] W. F. Muhammad was primed to redeem his father's brother following the customs of West African Muslims who often redeemed their enslaved relatives from the Americas' when they were made aware of a location whether it was in Brazil or North Carolina.

[20] AKA W. D. Fard

14. His own self is a righteous Muslim.
15. Are there any Muslims other than righteous?
16. I beg your pardon. I have never heard of one.
17. How many Muslim sons are there in North American?
18. Approximately three million.
19. How many original Muslims are there in North America?
20. A little over seventeen million.
21. Did I hear you say that some of the seventeen million do not know that they are Muslims?
22. YES SIR.
23. I hardly believe that unless they are blind, deaf and dumb.
24. Well, they were made blind, deaf and dumb by the devil when they were babies.
25. CAN THE DEVIL FOOL A MUSLIM?
26. NOT NOWADAYS.
27. Do you mean to say the devil fooled them three hundred seventy-nine years ago?
28. Yes, the TRADER made an interpretation that they receive GOLD for their labor, more then they were earning in their own country.
29. Then did they receive gold?
30. NO. The Trader disappeared and there was no one that could speak their language.
31. Then what happened?
31. WELL, they wanted to go to their own country, but they could not swim nine thousand miles.
32. Why didn't their own people come and get them?
33. Because their own people did not know that they were here.
34. When did there own people find out that they were here?
36. Approximately sixty years ago.

After accomplishing this Lesson No. C1, at once ask for Lesson No. C2 which will bring you a profit of $10.00 per word for studying it.

In conclusion, the current capital city of the Nation of Islam in North America is Chicago, Ill. Its intelligence stems primarily from the Supreme Wisdom Book and The Honorable Minister Louis Farrakhan—current head of the Nation of Islam.

In politics, a capital is the principal city or town associated with its government. It is almost always the city; which physically encompasses the offices and meeting places of the seat of government and fixed by law. The word capital is derived from the <u>Latin</u> caput meaning "head", and the related term capitol refers to the building where government-business is chiefly conducted. The nature of government responsibilities and its business is as follows:

Government
Administration of Educational Programs
Administration of General Economic Programs
Administration of Public Health Programs
Administration of Social, Human Resource and Income Maintenance Programs
Administration of Veterans' Affairs, Except Health Insurance
Air and Water Resource and Solid Waste Management
Correctional Institutions
Courts
Executive Offices
Executive and Legislative Offices, Combined
Fire Protection

General Government, NEC
International Affairs
Land, Mineral, Wildlife, and Forest Conservation
Legal Counsel and Prosecution
Legislative Bodies
Police Protection
Public Finance, Taxation, and Monetary Policy
Public Order and Safety, NEC
Regulation and Administration of Communications, Electric, Gas, and Other Utilities
Regulation and Administration of Transportation Programs
Regulation of Agricultural Marketing and Commodities

| Regulation, Licensing, and Inspection of Miscellaneous | Commercial Sectors United States Postal Service |

Today with a new generation of black professionals, politicians and entrepreneurs rising, their greatest test is whether or not they will become equipped to operate a networking socio-economic political *intranational* structure. I reiterate; the Asian community is achieving an example of such realities. They have not only built an *intranational* structure (nation within a nation inside of America), they did it by establishing a network of businesses within black communities employing the principles of family, hard work, love, education and concentrated negotiations with the capital of the U.S. government.

The days of blaming white America are very nearly useless! Thus, I quote the Finder of the members of the Lost and Found Nation of Islam in North America, Wallace Fard Muhammad:

"Don't tell her that there was no one to teach you for three hundred and seventy -nine years. She (America) already knows and is trying to forget it. Now she will teach you quickly any course you may desire." [21]

Quote by: Wallace Fard Muhammad, Problem #12

---

[21] Review Problem 12 on page 18.

Chapter 6

Instructions Given To The Labors

In this chapter, it will be demonstrated how Wallace Fard Muhammad referenced a future death plot that would advance against the life of his MESSENGER, Elijah Muhammad. This plot was written in the Supreme Wisdom Book under footnote 2: "Instructions Given to the Labors." It reads:

> "...According to the Holy Quran 59:7, the Muslims were very poor when they first started to Teach ISLAM and all contribution was given to Allah's Apostle for him and his family's Support. And what the Apostle could spare, he gave to help take care of the Poor Muslims that were unable to help themselves and the other was given to those who were confined to the Labor of ISLAM. And soon, there arose an argument among the Hypocrites about the use of the money...The enemy, then tried to stop every Muslim from helping the **Apostle** and said **he should be killed**. Then Allah Challenged the enemy to do so, to leave not a stone unturned in trying. This is in the 34 Problems that you have if you understand..."

To figure out the exact year when the enemy would seek to kill Elijah Muhammad (in this case, the Apostle), we must reexamine:

1) Statement No. 3 of English Lesson C1
2) Problem No. 32
3) Problem No. 31

English Lesson C1, statement No. 3 reads:

"My uncle was brought over here by the Trader *three hundred seventy-nine years ago.*"

So let's begin by subtracting 379 years from the time of the completion of the Supreme Wisdom Book.... 1934 minus 379 years equals 1555. The year 1555 is the point in time when Captain Sir John Hawkins[22] brought the first African slaves to James Town, Virginia.

Problem No. 32 reads:

"Now, the Messenger and his Labors worked day and night for the last three and one-half years, and their accomplishment is approximately twenty-five thousand. **The Messenger and his Labors are worried, for the time of Laboring is mentioned and limited in said, Problem No. 31.***"*

As you can see, W. F. Muhammad refers you back to Problem No. 31 to see "limited time" that the Messenger (Apostle) and his Labors had to work.

Problem No. 31 reads:

*"**A lion in a cage walks** back and forth, **sixty feet per minute**, seeking a way out of the cage. It took nearly **four centuries to find the door**. Now, with **modern equipment**, he is **walking three thousand feet per minute** and he has **three thousand miles by two thousand miles to go yet**. How long will it take him to cover this territory of said, three thousand by two thousand miles, at the above walking rate? Five thousand two hundred eight feet equals one mile."*

---

[22] First slaves were brought to North America on a slave ship named "Jesus of Lubeck" or "The Good ship Jesus" purchased by King Henry VIII. www.History of Sir John Hawkins.

To reveal the *"Messengers"* (Apostle) limited time of laboring up to the year when his enemies would seek to kill him, we must resolve the mathematical *parable of Problem No. 31* in two sets of calculations:

3,000 ft. per min. ÷ 5,280 ft. (1 mile) = .5681 ft. per mile

.5681 ft. per mile x 1,440 min. (1 day) = 818.064 ft.per day

818.064 ft. per day x 365 days = 298,593.36 ft. per year

3000 x 2000 miles = 6,000,000 miles

6,000,000 miles ÷ 298,593.36 ft. per year = 20.0 years

From these calculations, it took *"the Messenger"* 20 years to *"walk"* 6,000,000 miles, at 3,000 by 2,000 ft. per minute, "using modern equipment" before the death plot was unleashed. (20 years + 1955 = 1975) By this I mean, in year 1975, as Elijah Muhammad was convalescing at a hospital in Mexico, someone authorized him to be removed from the hospital, flown out of Mexico to Chicago where he was admitted into Chicago's Mercy Hospital.

Curiously, it was not until the 3rd month (March 21) of the year 1975 when funeral services were held for Elijah Muhammad at Mount Glenwood Cemetery, in Thornton, Illinois. Since when does it take three months to bury anyone? This may explain why we need a second calculation as demonstrated below, but in rounded figures only.

*3,000 ft. per min. ÷ 5,280 ft. (1 mile) = .57 ft.
per mile*

*.57 ft. per mile x 1,414 min. [23] (1 day) = 806 ft.
per day*

*806 ft. per day x 365 days = 294,190 ft.
per year*

3000 x 2000 miles = 6,000,000 miles

*6,000,000 miles ÷ 294,190 ft. per year = 20.3 (20
yrs, 3 months: March 1975)*

As we close the subject of a death plot, it is only fitting to provide a portion of an interview given in 1972 by one of the grandson's of Elijah Muhammad speaking to how another leader of the Nation of Islam would be chosen.

> *"This is in keeping with his, Elijah Muhammad's, statement to the press in 1972, there in his home, 4847 South Woodlawn Avenue, Chicago. "His statement, when ask by the press for a direct statement as to who his successor would be, was that God would choose his successor. That is to say that a messenger of God, as he put it, does not get into the business of choosing a messenger, for he is chosen by God," the grandson reported.*

> *(Source: Muhammad Speaks Newspaper March 21, 1975)*

I make no interpretation as to whether or not Elijah Muhammad escaped a death plot in 1975. As you have read, his Master Teacher, Wallace Fard Muhammad, mathematically prefigured it in what is called ***"Instructions Given To The Labors"*** by

---

[23] The actual hours per day is 23.5646 times 60 minutes equal 1,413.876 minutes per day. Rounded off is 1,414 minutes.

directing the reader to search the 34 Problems of the "Problem Book". However, the foremost international witness who has stated publicly *"Elijah Muhammad did escape a death plot"* is Minister Louis Farrakhan Muhammad—the most vibrant registered Muslim of the Nation of Islam in North America for now 51 years.

To reveal Minister Farrakhan's value as a registered member of the N.O.I., one must further clarify the esoteric, metaphoric and mathematical parable of Problem No. 31 by reckoning the 400 years *"it took the Lion to find the door"* from the time when the first slaves landed in James Town, Virginia. (1555 + 400 years = 1955) The significance of year 1955 within the context of the Supreme Wisdom Book relates to Louis Farrakhan (a.k.a. Louis Gene Walcott) who joined the Nation of Islam that year to become a Laborer for *Messenger Elijah Muhammad*. Was Louis Gene Walcott the little helper whom the "*Messenger*" desired as he mentioned during a Saviours Day speech in 1954:

"Since you and me are witnesses here this afternoon in this world that we live, we have been so greatly misunderstood that I desire that Allah send to me a little helper; for 22 years I have worked hard wherever I was or may be to try to get into your ears and into your hearts the truth that Allah has revealed to me."

If we subtract 22 years from 1954, this meant *Messenger Elijah Muhammad* was looking for a little helper since 1932. Obviously *Fard* told him that he would need a helper. Why else would Elijah say he had been looking for a helper for 22 years? He was not dealing in guesswork. He was dealing with science, mathematics, scripture, theology and the "mysterious knowledge" contained within The Supreme Wisdom Book.

Saviours Day 1955

The next year—on February 26th, 1955—the year that marked the fulfillment of the 400 year prophesy that we were to serve our enemies (Genesis 15), the Honorable Elijah Muhammad was divinely given that sign. He recognized that *special* helper who was sitting in the audience and at once gave him the essence of his assignment.[24] I reiterate, in 1955 Louis Gene Walcott entered to door of the Nation of Islam attending his first Saviours Day convention on February 26, 1955. After he joined, he was the first "modernly equipped" registered Muslim with three years of college education. He not only ran track, but also majored in English. Louis Gene Walcott was the proverbial

Lion in the cage who found the door, into the N.O.I.... just the human being whom Elijah Muhammad needed to help him particularly after year 1975.

Community of Jesus

The Muslim book of scripture, Holy Quran, reveals the community of Jesus will be made greater than all communities at the end of the world. It reads, *"When Allah said: O Jesus, I will cause thee to die (sleep) and exalt thee in My presence and clear thee of those who disbelieve and make those who follow thee above those who disbelieve to the day of Resurrection. Then to Me is your return, so I shall decide between you concerning that wherein you differ" (Quran 3:55)*

Islamic prophet, *Prophet Mohammed ibn Abdullah of Arabia,* made his interpretation about the above prophetic verse 1,400 years ago. He said:

---

[24] By Jabril Muhammad Updated May 13, 2008 Final Call Newspaper

"How will you (Muslims) be when Jesus, the son of Mary descends amongst you and he will judge people by the Law of the Quran and not the Gospel...there will be no taxation taken from non-Muslims as to avoid embracing Islam...all people will embrace Islam...Money will be in abundance."[25]

It is my belief that war has always been about control over currency (resources) and its application of wealth distribution. In fact, husbands and wives of the smallest households dispute to control resources. The question becomes: Will the people legislating "economic" laws abide by Quranic financial sciences or Gospel financial sciences or a little of both. Whomever you think it should be, it appears that Muslims are expecting the *community of Jesus* to take control of the financial principles for wealth distribution, including reforming the tax conundrum used worldwide!

Fact is Black Americans, including the Nation of Islam, Latino's; Mexican's, Native American's and others of goodwill represent the community of Jesus. If only we might employ the financial laws of the Quran to legislate an *Econometric formula* to free humanity from unjust usury debt, change is possible. Provided each one put aside their childish theological allegorical dogma, change cannot be choked-out.

Additionally Christian Black America must inspire great numbers of their young men and women to become qualified in the area of how to employ currency into service for public use as it is meant. You may have read, the Bible is clear on three legal money principles: (1) monetary debasement is wrong (Isaiah 1:22); (2) multiple indebtedness, which is the basis of

---

[25] Footnote: Holy Quran 3:55, see page 76 of "Noble Quran" by Dr. Muhammad Taqi-ud Din Al Hilali and Dr. Muhammad Muhsin Khan.

fractional reserve banking, must not be allowed (Exodus 22:26); and (3) weights and measures must not be tampered with (Lev. 19:36). Regrettably modern economic policy-makers diabolically violate all three.

Financial Reform

A major reform in the area of "money-science" is in demand. The great Zionist banking families of old Europe very well understand the plight of their money system which has positioned Europeans as the "God-Fathers" of Finance for more than 300 years. England's reign as a world power actually began on Threadneedle Street. Then, no bank had its own building and bankers were but goldsmiths who lent money and rented space to do business. But after the moneylenders cut their bargain (and it was a bargain) with King William of England, things were never to be the same, either for England or the moneylenders—or the world. In 1694, by bailing King William out of his debts incurred by England 's war with France, the moneylenders achieved enormous power and a new found respectability. They now called themselves bankers and would profit by the vast sums of credit that were to underwrite the greatest empire since imperial Rome —an era that is now about to end....

England ultimately leveraged its ability to wage war with credit into a world empire; and, the moneylenders, now called bankers, used England's power to spread their system of credit-based money across the world, multiplying and increasing their profits thereby.

When the US succeeded England as a world power, the bankers instituted the same system of debt-based money in the US but with very different results. Now in 2008, after three centuries of fueling economic expansion, the magic of the moneychangers has reached its limits. The end of an epoch is at hand.[26] Today's rulers of the credit monopoly understand a more equitable principle of wealth distribution must come to pass if they are to survive economically. If they think by purposely collapsing the system and then revive it, as it was done in 1929 they are doomed. It won't work thanks to the Buddhist of Asia. The only way to survive is DO THE RIGHT THING, if you have the nature to do so.

In fact, Global Student Experience, a California Corporation offer an introduction course to the economic systems and social policies of the five largest Western European nations: Germany, France, the United Kingdom, Spain, and Italy. In this course, these five countries, all members of the European Union, are compared to determine whether a "Western European" model of economic and social development has emerged. To the degree that such a model exists, the question will be raised whether it can survive in changing world economic conditions.[27]

If and when the Western European economic models crumbles, at last, China, India, Arabia and other third world nations have finally produced enough offspring to engage the Western worlds money-science matrix; and, soon South America. However, if the real community of Jesus engage and excel in this system by employing the economic principles of Quranic law, according to Prophet Mohammed's tax reform agenda and the Biblical economic principles, all nations will be freed from unnecessary debt and oppression from our current banking establishment.

---

[26] http://www.marketoracle.co.uk/Article3325.html

[27] www.gseabroad.com/cd-8221_cityID-7.aspx

Free to enjoy the rule of law, life, liberty and the pursuit of happiness! The question is: Will the real community of Jesus qualify themselves and act to reform the science of fractional reserve banking and usury? Or will enunciations of religious allegorical dogma full of symbolisms without substance continue.

Chapter 7

Application of Supreme Wisdom Book

The six sets of lessons of the Supreme Wisdom Book is not useless knowledge except if it's not applied. The content of its message was designed first for memorization, then cryptanalysis and finally fulfillment. Of course, one can mull over the formality of its raw material of words, letters, and numbers. However, in today's age of technology and information it would accomplish nothing without attainment.

The following quote by Mr. Elijah Muhammad was to the early Muslims of 1937. His quote evinces the above view as conclusive:

> *"...Have we entered number two lesson, where Wise hidden wisdom relating to this day of our is? Have we clearly understood the Forms, and the knowledge of ACTUAL FACTS?...*
>
> *No man will begin a building without the actual facts concerning its measurements nor without a square or compass and a plumb line. This he must have to make a form to begin his building..."*[28]

The Supreme Wisdom Book is designed to direct its Learner to think of a variety of courses and actions to take toward freedom and self-reliance. For instance:

---

[28] (Source Muhammad Speaks Newspaper: Written and sent to all students in the University of Islam in the Wilderness of North America April 3, 1937 By: Elijah Muhammad, Servant of ALLAH)

a) *Supreme Wisdom Book, Actual Fact #14 states*: The producing land is 29,000,000 square miles.

Field of Study: Agronomics

b) *Area of Study*: Study of productivity of land

c) *Derived Industry*: Soybeans (**soybean industry**)

d) *Economic (or social benefit) potential*: (1) 2005 72.1 million acres planted, (2) $16 Billion Farm cash receipts and production, (3) 435 million bushels exported to China. (4) Employment (5) Grocery Store (6) Shipping and trucking (7) etc., etc.

 e) *Educational requirements*: Mathematics, Physical Life Science, Agricultural Science, Economics, Biology, Principles of Crop Production, etc;

Another example of how The Supreme Wisdom Book directs its Learner to think of what courses and actions to take toward freedom and self-reliance may be stimulated by Problem 11. For example:

a) *Supreme Wisdom Book Problem #11*: The Suez Canal in Egypt is ninety miles long, with a depth of thirty-three feet, and a width of one hundred twenty-two feet. The cost to build it sixty-four years ago was one hundred fifty million dollars. Mr. A. Ali has five hundred dollars worth of *stock* in it at the rate of six and three-fifths percent. Now he wants to know how much money he has coming to him at the above rate from 1869 to May 26, 1933…

 Field of Study: catalactics

b) *Area of Study*: science of commercial exchange

c) *Derived Industries*: International Banks, Commercial Banks, Public Banks, Stock exchange, etc;

d) **_Economic (or social benefit) potential_**: (1) Holistic Intranationalism...(2) Friedrich Hayek used the term Catallaxy to describe a market economy. He was unhappy with the usage of the word "economy", feeling that the Greek root of the word - which translates as "household management" - implied that economic agents in a market economy possessed shared goals. Hayek derived the word Catallaxy from the Greek verb "katallassein" (or "katallattein") which meant not only "to exchange" but also "to admit in the community" and "to change from enemy into friend" (F.A. von Hayek, Law legislation and Liberty, Vol 2, 1976, pp. 108-109).

Lastly, the word **_Stock_** mentioned in Problem #11 opens up an entire world. The stock market directs ones mind to the science of **_catalactics_** (science of commercial exchange), if he or she is made aware of such a field of study. It also may direct ones mind to **_notaphilly_** (collecting of bank-notes) and how it affects the security and stability of any Money Matrix System. To transport these sciences into a reality begin with offspring who are trained, educated and groomed to establish national, intranational and global financial mechanisms to bring about economy. Although stock exchanges do not exist to redistribute wealth; however, both casual and professional stock investors, through dividends and stock price increases that may result in capital gains, will share in the wealth of profitable businesses. Or at least this is what they should do.

All governments need a money matrix system, which means it needs a "priesthood" of financial wizards. The basic entry qualification to produce such a "priesthood" require applicants who must have specialized experience and/or directly related education in the amounts shown below:

81

e) *Education requirements*:

Accounting *4 years*
Auditing *2 years*
Avertising & Market Strategy *1 year*
Economics *4 years*
Laws & Taxation *4 years*
Foreign Language *2 years*
Foreign Trade Statics *4 years*
Mathematics *4 years*
Risk Management *4 years*
Production Market Research *4 years*
Interest & Exchange Rates *4 years*
Welfare & Reform *2 years*
Outsourcing *1 years*
Globalization *2 years*
Anti-trust Merging *4 years*
Commodity while dealing with stock and bond *4 years*
Mathematics *4 years*
Researching *2 years*
Investing *4 years*
Merging *4 years*
Signatures, Autographs, and Age *1 year*
Condition and Rarity *1 year*

In conclusion, building an *intranational* government, a nation within a nation, is not trouble-free. It takes unyielding faith in Divine Omni Presence, obedience to good quality authority and obedience to the academic discipline of the sciences to maintain a nation.

Acknowledgment

And certainly We have made the Word to have many connections for their sake, so that they maybe mindful. Those to whom We gave the Book before it, they are believers in it. And when it is recited to them they say: We believe in it; surely it is the Truth from our Lord; we were indeed before this submitting ones." –Holy Qur'an, Surah 28, verses 51-53

I thank Allah, the originator of the Heavens and the Earth. I also thank Wallace Fard Muhammad for coming to America in the early 1930's to relegate Elijah Muhammad's assignment of establishing Islam to engineer justice for and among Black people in North America. I thank his Servant, Elijah Muhammad and those early Labors, Ministers, Captains, Lieutenants and believers for working to lay a foundation for new generations to build upon.

I thank Minister Louis Farrakhan for making the Supreme Wisdom Book of Lessons accessible for all to see, read, study, decipher and implement over the last fifteen years, since 1991. I also thank Brother Jabril Muhammad and Mother Tynetta Muhammad for inspiring me to study years ago. Thanks too Allah for my father, Ali Rasheed for helping me to resolve problem No. 31. of the Supreme Wisdom Book. Brother Ali, a one time registered Muslim of the Nation of Islam, prior to 1975, was very gratified to have read, for the first time, the entire text of the Supreme Wisdom Book. Prior to 1975, ninety-five percent of all registered Muslims only received portions of it. For the most part, only top laborers and officials had access to all six lessons. Thanks to Allah for brother Stanley Muhammad (former Minster of Mosque #54). I was talking to him about the lessons when the idea came to me to write this book. Thanks also to brother Philip Muhammad (of Mosque #27 and western region Final Call distributor) for advising me how to edit chapter six of this book. Again, thanks to sister Aiesha Muhammad (student minister of Mosque #32 of Phoenix, Arizona) for suggesting that I give this book a broader title and appeal and thanks to sister Brittney X Tane' of Portland, Oregon for her research into lesson 11 of the Problem Book. Lastly, I thank Sultan Muhammad for giving Minister Louis Farrakhan a copy of this book to review in early 2007.

Lastly, I thank Allah for permitting me to see the fields of study--ologies fixed within the Supreme Wisdom Book of Lessons. For without remembrance of Him, this book would not have been possible.